GETTING
LITTLE
BLIGHTERS
TO
BEHAVE

The dos and don'ts of keeping
your kids on your side

CLAIRE POTTER

Illustrated by Mark Beech

FEATHERSTONE

LONDON OXFORD NEW YORK NEW DELHI SYDNEY

To Jimbo, the biggest blighter in the whole family
(the one with the brizzles and the big tentacles)

FEATHERSTONE
Bloomsbury Publishing Plc
50 Bedford Square, London, WC1B 3DP, UK
BLOOMSBURY, FEATHERSTONE and the Feather logo are trademarks of Bloomsbury Publishing Plc

First published in Great Britain 2018 by Bloomsbury Publishing Plc

A catalogue record for this book is available from the British Library

ISBN: PB: 978-1-4729-4674-4; ePDF: 978-1-4729-4590-7; ePub: 978-1-4729-6534-9

2 4 6 8 10 9 7 5 3 1

Text design by Cathy Tincknell

Printed and bound by CPI Group (UK) Ltd., Croydon, CR0 4YY

All papers used by Bloomsbury Publishing Plc are natural, recyclable products from wood grown in well
managed forests. The manufacturing processes conform to the environmental regulations of the country
of origin

To find out more about our authors and books visit www.bloomsbury.com and sign up for our newsletters

CONTENTS

Introduction

When I look back at the childhood of my eldest son (now 18, all grown-up with a salary and saucepan set of his own), I remember it all fondly. Even the really naughty incidents – like the time he threw all our passports out the window on a wet and windy day or painted our white garden chairs with black bitumen paint – bring a smile to my face! But they definitely weren't funny at the time.

The reality is that when we're in the thick of raising our children, day in, day out, their behaviour can often get in the way of us fully enjoying them. Those little legs don't seem quite so cute when they're running away in the wrong direction. That picture of a cat they've drawn isn't quite so wonderful when they've done it on the kitchen table instead of the paper.

Wouldn't it be great to have children who behaved (most of the time) in a way that meant we could enjoy them to the max, right here, right now? I set out to find out how.

I met with child psychologists to squeeze the knowledge and expertise from their brains. I wanted to know what we can do that will actually make a difference to our children's behaviour. What does the evidence show? What *really* works? Then I carefully sifted and sorted, shaped and squashed the information I collected into one little book that even the most frazzled parent could read in less than one and a half cups of tea or a large glass of wine at the end of another challenging day.

'Sometimes when I see a mum on the bus on my way to work really struggling with her child's behaviour,' said one of the child psychologists I interviewed, 'I just want to go over and tell her one thing that would really help... but I can't.' This is a book full of those things.

Wishing you a happy, harmonious time with your little blighters!

Claire Potter

Note

It is important that you seek professional help in any of the following cases:
- Your child is completely out of control.
- Your child seems to show no empathy at all.
- Your child is cruel to animals.
- You are frightened of your child.

1 Give them a regular top-up of attention

Kids crave our attention. It's as simple as that! And if we don't give it to them voluntarily, they'll seek it in ways we don't like. *Aha! Got your full attention now, haven't I?* they think, as you tell them off for smearing baby's nappy cream all over your iPad®!

That's not to say you should be giving them your full attention every single waking moment of their day. Of course not! There are three different 'modes' of interacting with your child and a mix of all three is quite normal and natural.

Mode 1: No attention – you're doing something else and not responding to your child at all, e.g. making an important phone call or on the toilet!

Mode 2: Half attention – you're responding to your child but you're doing or thinking about something else at the same time, e.g. cooking dinner or on social media.

Mode 3: Full attention – you're fully focused on your child and not being distracted by anything or anyone else, e.g. you're playing a game with them or watching a 'show' they've made up.

The problem is that in our often manic, multi-tasking, smartphone-driven lives, it's all too easy to pass the whole day in a blur of only Modes 1 and 2. And if this happens day after day, it will lead to difficult behaviour. Children need bursts of Mode 3!

When your child knows there are periods of your time that are entirely set aside for them, they are much more likely to behave well when they're not getting – or only half getting – your attention.

'Mum... Mum... Muuuuuuum!'

Sometimes your child will demand your full attention — immediately! It helps if you respond quickly (at the 'Mum' stage) rather than waiting until they feel ignored and disgruntled ('Muuuuuuum!'). That doesn't mean you have to drop everything to attend to them but make it very clear what mode you're in, e.g. 'I AM listening to you but I have to make the packed lunches at the same time' or 'Give me ten minutes to finish this email and then I'll be with you'. Then stick to what you say — even if they've wandered off and got involved in something else. Don't make them wait until you've finished the email, paid three bills and hoovered the floor! If you do, they'll stop believing their time will come and won't let you get on with what you're doing.

If this hasn't been happening regularly it can take a little time to see a turnaround in your child's behaviour, but when it's in place, it's super-effective. Even as little as 10 minutes in a day can make a difference.

Obviously, the make-up of your family — one parent or two, one child or five — will affect how much and how often your child can have your full attention. There are no hard and fast rules. A session playing with a three-year-old before you pick your older child up from school may work wonders, whereas a ten-year-old may be satisfied that day with a cosy chat after their younger siblings have gone to bed. Activities or games where all the family are involved give a boost too, especially if you let each child have a turn at choosing what you do together.

Think of it as topping up their attention 'credit' levels — to keep them running smoothly when your attention is not available.

QUICK TIP

Have you ever presented your child with a new toy or activity and thought 'Da-nah! There, that'll keep you occupied for a while' — only to find they still pester for your attention? Even a whole room bursting with shiny, new, exciting toys can be less precious to your child than your attention. If you spend just a little time exploring the new toy or activity with them to get them interested and involved, it can really pay off!

2 Let them lead the way with play

So you've got 10, 20, 45 or even a 100 uninterrupted minutes to devote to your child. What's the best thing to do with them?

When you have some free time to play with your child, let them be in the driving seat. The effect on their overall behaviour can be striking.

This is how it works. First off, your child gets to choose what you do together. For instance, you might say, *I have half an hour. Let's do something, just you and me. What would you like to do?*

Oh boy, I hear you groan. *But they'll make me move around Playmobil® figures and do their voices... Play Hedbanz again... Push them round the garden in the wheelbarrow...* [insert activity you really dislike!]. Yes, it can be really tedious. In fact, it's often what stops us throwing ourselves into playing with our child. We'll scroll through Facebook at the same time or even sidle off to defrost the freezer! But if you grin and bear it, the payback can be big.

When you know they're likely to choose something that will take too long or be too stressful for you right now (getting the paints out... putting the tent up in the garden...),

you can limit it up front by asking them to suggest two or three things from which you can choose. And if they're already very happily involved in something, you can simply join in.

But let's say your child says, *I want to build a Lego® skyscraper with you.* The second important thing to know is that they also get to be top dog throughout the activity itself. The natural, instinctive thing as a parent is to guide and instruct your child. *We need to straighten up this wall,* you might say or, *Doesn't it need some windows?*

Resist! Maybe they don't want any windows and maybe they don't mind the wonky wall. Follow their lead entirely. Be at your child's whim!

If they go off at a tangent – the plan was to build a skyscraper, but now you're building a giraffe, or the plan was to play draughts but now they want to see how many of the pieces they can balance on their nose – that's okay too. Don't say, *I thought we were building a skyscraper* or *Come on, let's get on with the game.* There doesn't need to be an end point. In fact, there doesn't need to be a point at all! It's only the attention and the togetherness that matter – and will make a difference to their behaviour.

Make like a sports commentator!

A good way to talk to your child when you're playing with them is to imagine you're commenting on a football match – only instead of 'What a fantastic strike' or 'It's a corner', you might say things like 'That train's going all the way through the tunnel' or 'You're colouring in the mermaid's tail purple'. Simply observe and describe what they're doing. This not only stops you taking charge, it makes your child feel special and 100% focused on. You may actually see them swell with pleasure before your eyes!

QUICK TIP

Conversation counts as attention too if that's what your child chooses – as long as you really tune in and listen fully with lots of 'mmms' and 'arrrs'. There might be nothing duller than hearing every detail of a computer game, for example, but go with it. Just as you'd sit and listen to a friend tell you something they'd told you three times before!

3 Catch them doing something good!

A dad was moaning to his sister on the phone about his son's behaviour. *He's ALWAYS looking for trouble* he complained. *He NEVER just sits still and gets on with something,* he said. *Oh dear,* she replied. *What's he doing at the moment?* The dad stopped to think. *Now?... erm... he's playing with his trains.*

When you're struggling with your child's behaviour, it's so easy to get into a negative mindset and completely overlook the bits when they're behaving well. But as a parent, attention really is your super-power, your magic wand — and now is the very best time to wave it!

Start spotting the good things — however tiny and infrequent they are — and pounce with some positive attention. If you get into the habit of this, the behaviours you want to see will gradually increase.

If your child, who is sometimes aggressive towards you, comes up and gives you a spontaneous cuddle, you could say, *I love it when you do that.* If your child, who finds it difficult to share, offers another child a go with their favourite toy, you could say, *Nice sharing.* Maybe the boy playing with his trains was difficult the entire rest of the day — but that's all the more reason to 'catch' him when he's being easy! *Ooh, that's a great train track you made there while I was on the phone. Look at that!*

The positive attention you give your child doesn't have to be praise. It could be a simple *Thank you,* a thumbs up or a shoulder squeeze. It could be taking five minutes to let them talk you through the picture they drew while you were putting the shopping away, or joining in when they're playing happily with their play dough

---

The art of giving praise

You may have heard that praise is more powerful if it's specific — that instead of vague, throwaway comments like 'Good girl' or 'Well done', you should tell your child exactly why you're pleased with them, e.g. 'That's great that you came straight in and hung your coat up on the peg like that' (to a child who normally throws their coat on the floor). This is true, but the words coming out your mouth should feel natural. If they're going to sound clunky and fake (Why is daddy talking like that?!), a 'Well done' (with eye contact and a nod to the peg in this case) will be just fine!

after they'd been moaning they were bored. Anything that makes your child feel you have noticed and are happy with what they are doing will powerfully reinforce that behaviour.

Don't go over the top though – or it could backfire! If they give their friend one of their new stickers out of a pack of a 100 and you lay it on thick about how incredibly kind and generous they are, it could come across as insincere, patronising or manipulative. *It really wasn't a very big deal,* they'll think. *Why is she acting like it is?* It'll make them feel less, not more, inclined to want to repeat that behaviour. They may even want to rebel. *If it's such a big deal, let's see how much attention it gets me get if I don't do it!* For the same reason, once the new behaviour becomes the norm, ease off and just occasionally pay positive attention to it to keep them on track.

With time, you really will see lasting changes. Be positive about the positive!

QUICK TIP

When you praise your child, resist a little dig about what they did wrong before! 'Well done for putting your shoes on when I asked – why can't you always do that?' or 'Thank you for brushing your hair – about time too!' The human brain receives and processes negativity more acutely than positivity, so it will come across as criticism rather than praise.

4 Ignore the bad stuff

What your child most wants is your positive attention – but if they can't get that they'll settle for your negative attention. They'd much rather you told them off than didn't notice them at all.

Take this case of a mother boarding a train with her happy toddler in a buggy. The mum gets out her phone. After a few minutes, her toddler looks up at her, points to another train whooshing past and giggles. The mum half looks up briefly but doesn't smile or say anything. After another minute or two, the toddler starts kicking at her seat. The mum takes her eyes off her phone, looks right at him and says sharply, *No! Don't do that!*

What is the child learning? I get way more attention when I do the bad stuff! She's waving her wand at the wrong time!

Just as giving positive attention to positive behaviours makes those behaviours grow, giving negative attention to negative behaviours makes those grow too. Starve them of attention instead until they shrivel and disappear.

So how do we put this into action?

First of all, let's take those niggly – but harmless – little things that children do to get a reaction from you: flicking food on the floor, making farting noises at you, trying out a swear word... These things can be totally ignored. Avert your gaze, gently remove any offending object and carry on doing what you were doing.

However, if your child does something aggressive or destructive, take the ignoring to a higher level. Suppose your child throws a piece of a board

Tackling a tantrum

What's the quickest way to stop a tantrum? Ignore it. Even in a public place – embarrassing as it is – doing anything else will only make it last longer. Here's the dos and don'ts:

• Don't call it a tantrum – if it becomes a 'thing' with a name, it gains more power in your child's mind.

• Don't try to talk or reason with your child. It's pointless. In this heightened state of emotion, they can't process what you're saying or think logically.

• Start by acknowledging their emotions, e.g. 'I can see you're really angry about this'. (The tantrum may be unacceptable but their emotion is still real.) Then turn your back or take a few steps away. Say 'When you're cross it's difficult for us to talk but I'm here when you're ready'. Leave them until they've calmed down by themselves.

• Afterwards, stick to your guns. If you give in to what they wanted, they'll learn to switch on a tantrum to get their own way even when there's no genuine anger or upset behind it.

game at you in frustration because they're losing. *No, it's not okay to throw things at me,* you can say calmly (showing anger or annoyance would be attention). *I'm going to stop playing now. I'll play again when you're ready to play nicely.* Stay where you are but physically turn away from your child.

If it happens again, take it to the next level. Say (still calmly), *I told you it's not okay to throw things at people. I'm not going to play until you stop.* Then take yourself to the other side of the room and get on with something else.

The aim isn't to punish your child by making yourself emotionally unavailable. You simply want to give them the message: *I engage with you when you do THESE things and not when you do THOSE things.*

So the instant your child stops the behaviour – even if it's a switch from anger to upset or a subtle change of subject like asking for a drink – bounce straight back in with some positive attention that shows them *Yay! This is the behaviour we want.*

> **QUICK TIP**
> When your child does something that makes you so angry you feel you might say or do something unkind or threatening to them, the best thing you can do (as long as your child is safe) is walk away. You can say, 'I'm so angry right now that I have to be on my own for a bit. I'll talk to you when I've calmed down'. Then go to a different room or space.

5 Put them in the picture

Imagine this. You're in the middle of watching your favourite TV programme. Totally absorbed. In the moment. *Get your coat on then,* says your partner popping their head round the door. *The film starts at 8.30.* He disappears. *Huh?* you think. *You didn't tell me we were going out.* You probably wouldn't be very receptive to the idea, would you?!

Yet, so often we expect our children to jump when we say jump without any warning at all. Perhaps we're busy getting ready ourselves. Perhaps we assume they've already gleaned what's happening or that they don't need to know – they'll know soon enough. But children are no different from us in this way. If we spring something on them, we're much more likely to meet resistance.

Come and have your bath! we might call out of the blue when they're completely engrossed in colouring a picture. *Noooooo!* they shout. *I want to finish this.* They're reluctant. You push. They resist. You insist. They refuse. It escalates into a row.

Your child will be much more willing to co-operate if they know what's coming in advance. It gives them the chance to mentally prepare themselves.

It also makes them feel included and respected, instead of like a puppet on a string. (After all, how many times when they're finally ready do we then say, *Oh, hang on a minute…* and go off and do something else?!).

You may already be familiar with the idea of giving your child a five-minute warning before you leave the park or a play date, but we need to extend this to other situations too. So tell them you're about to run their bath. Tell them in the morning if they're having a babysitter that evening and remind them again later. Tell them that you won't be able to go to the paddling pool as promised until the afternoon because you have to wait in for a delivery. Tell them that you're going to have to stop off at the supermarket on the way home to get a few things.

And if it's their first experience of something, describe to them what it'll be like so they know what to expect. First ever check-up at the dentist? Tell them about the big chair that goes backwards, the goggles and the 'pink water'. First time on a plane? Tell them about the whoosh of the plane along the runway for take-off, the bump of the landing and the meals in trays with little compartments. Give them the opportunity to look forward to things!

If they know and understand what's on the agenda, they'll be much happier to go along with it.

'Get a move on!'

When you find yourself hurrying your child along, it's worth stopping to ask yourself: 'Do I really need to rush them right now?' or 'Am I just being impatient?'. Things will go more smoothly if you go at your child's pace whenever you can. If you're on your way to feed the ducks and your child wants to stop and splash about in a big puddle, does it really matter if you don't make it any further than the puddle? If you're making cakes together and your child starts making smiley faces in the mixture, do you really need to move them on to the next step just yet? As adults, we often get fixated on the destination, the end point, but for your child – who is still exploring and learning about the world – the journey, the process, is just as interesting and important!

QUICK TIP
Units of time like 'another five minutes' don't mean a lot to a young child. They'll accept timings more readily if you word them in a way they can relate to. For instance, at the park: 'You've got time to go on one more thing – what are you going to choose?' Or in the car: 'It'll take us half an hour to get there – that's like one swimming lesson'.

6 Explain WHY

A mother and her two-and-a-half-year-old son were on a bus. The child reached out to press the red STOP button. *No!* said his mum, taking hold of his hand. *You mustn't touch that.* He tried again. *Stop it! That's naughty!* He reached for it yet again with a grin on his face. What a good game this was! *The driver will stop the bus and come and tell you off,* she resorted to.

Children will ignore or rebel against 'No!'s and instructions if they keep coming without an explanation. They are much more likely to co-operate if you tell them the reason why they should or shouldn't do something.

That button tells the driver that you want to get off the bus, you could say, *so you only press it when the bus is nearly at your bus stop. Look... that man is pressing it now... it makes that sign light up, see? It says 'Bus stopping'.*

Explaining the reason entices them to stay on the same side as you instead of setting up a them-and-you situation. It invites them into the grown-up world and explains how it works and how they can fit into it – and children are strongly programmed to want to learn this!

Let's look out the window, you can continue, *and when we see the fish and chip shop near our house, then YOU can press the button!*

It's so easy NOT to give them a reason. You might assume they already know why because it seems so obvious to you. You might think it's too complicated to explain to a child. You might be tired, busy or stressed. But it's worth it! The effort and energy it takes to give the reason is a lot less than the effort and aggravation of dealing with the behaviour that might follow if you don't.

Of course, the reason won't always be that interesting. Let's say your child wants to stop and play at the park. *We can't today because we have to be at the opticians at 2.30. If we're late, they might not be able to see us,* or *Sorry, there's frozen peas and fish fingers in the shopping and I need to get home quickly and put them in the freezer before they go all soft and mushy.*

Whatever the reason, you'll be facing the world side by side, instead of facing each other head-to-head.

BUS STOPPING

SIDE-EFFECT
Getting into the habit of giving an explanation makes you stop and think about why you're about to say 'No' and whether it's a good reason. Are you saying 'No' for no's sake? Are you being fair? Are you being overcautious? Are you in a bad mood about something else? Can you just not be bothered? You may actually decide you should allow your child to do what they asked to do after all.

7 Don't squash their emotions

> What are you making such a fuss for?

> Stop crying!

> It's nothing to worry about. It'll be fine.

Your child is playing with an elastic band on the way home from nursery school. It snaps. They start sobbing.

Don't be silly! It's just an elastic band, you say, trying to stop the tears as quickly as possible. *You can have another one when we get home. I've got loads in the drawer.*

But now your child cries even harder and stomps their feet. You seem to have made things worse, not better. Because however trivial a snapped elastic band seems to us as an adult, to your child at that moment it may genuinely feel like the worst thing in the world. *But that elastic band was really precious to me,* they're thinking. *Mummy just doesn't GET it.*

So what should you do instead? Here's the secret: instead of dismissing their emotions, zoom right in on them.

When you're in a tricky situation with your child because they're feeling angry, upset, frustrated, disappointed, worried or any other emotion, directly acknowledge what they're feeling. Head on!

Oh no, did your elastic band break? you'd say, getting down to their level.

Driven to distraction

Imagine your child is really cross because another child is playing with a toy digger they want to play with. They're about to peel the other child's hands off it. It's very tempting to try to distract them ('Ooh look, why don't you play with this lorry instead?'). This is a good tactic — but only if you acknowledge what they're feeling first. Otherwise you'll be teaching them to ignore or suppress their feelings, which is not healthy in the long-term. It's not actually the emotion we want to stop (it's okay to feel angry), only their reaction to the emotion (hand-peeling is not okay!).

I can see that's REALLY upset you. Believe it or not, you have a much higher chance of your child calming down quickly. In fact, the effect can be magical.

Just like you, your child wants to feel understood. They want to have their emotions recognised, not squashed. They want to receive empathy, not a quick fix. Imagine if someone said to you when you'd just burnt a hole with the iron in your favourite shirt: *Get over it. It's only a shirt. You can buy another one.*

So if your child is yelling at their sibling because they accidentally knocked down their marble run, instead of saying *Stop it! He didn't do it* on purpose – you can build it again, say: *I can see that was really annoying for you.* If your child is moaning and groaning about going to the doctor to have an injection, instead of saying *Oh, it'll be over really quickly and you can have an ice-cream afterwards,* say: *I can see you're feeling really worried about it.*

The more accurately you label their emotion, the more effective it will be. Are they angry or actually frustrated? Sad or more disappointed?

And that's all you have to do. Nothing more. There's no need to follow up with lots of questions (*Why was the elastic band so special to you?*). If you acknowledge their emotion, it will automatically give them the go-ahead to tell you more if they want to (*My friend Billy gave me that elastic band*). Don't jump in with solutions either. However, if they suggest their own (*Can you tie my elastic band back together?*) as long as it's easily doable, by all means go along with it!

THE BIG PICTURE
This technique also teaches your child empathy. If you're compassionate to them, they're more likely to be compassionate towards you and others. Win-win!

8 Cut them some slack

A young girl was with her mum in the lobby of a primary school waiting to pick up her big brother from an after-school club. To amuse herself, she started hopping from square to square on the carpet, counting how many hops she could do under her breath. *Stop doing that!* said her mum. *Come and stand next to me.* The girl persisted.

It's easy to chide and chivvy our children about things that really don't matter. If we're not careful, it can become a running commentary – like a really negative, never-ending game of Simon Says: *Leave that alone. Sit up properly. Stop fiddling with those...*

It might be because we're irritated by what they're doing. It might be because we're trying to keep them safe. It might be because we're worrying about what other people are thinking. We want our child to be – or at least seen to be! – under control at all times. But this kind of micromanaging can actually increase, not reduce, behaviour problems.

Why?

Firstly, it aggravates the child. Children want and need to be children – to explore, to experiment, to use their imagination – and a lot of these behaviours are just that. We shouldn't expect them to behave like mini-adults.

Secondly, if we continually bombard our children with commands, they will become 'deaf' to them, even the important ones. Your voice will become an incessant, annoying noise in their ear that they'll learn to zone out. They'll take less and less notice of what you say.

Thirdly, it sets up a battleground. Instead of keeping your child on the same side as you, endless reprimands invite them to be the opposition. So rather than co-operation, you're more likely to get resistance and rebellion.

Safe but not sound

We all want to keep our children safe, but we shouldn't try and protect them from every tiny thing. Do you really need to say 'Do your coat up properly' or could you leave it up to them to decide if they're cold? Is it fair to say 'Don't climb on that, it's too high!' even though it's a climbing frame built for kids? It's through experience and making mistakes that children learn to make good decisions for themselves, even if that means sometimes getting a bit cold or grazing a knee. Think of yourself as wide open arms within which your child is free to run, wriggle, dig, climb, trip and sometimes tumble. That's okay — you'll be there to pick them up.

On top of all that, your child won't be able to learn to distinguish between what's genuinely important and not very important at all, between right and wrong, between safe and dangerous. They need to gauge the difference between not touching a salt shaker in a café and not touching an electric fence, between drawing with their finger on the steamed-up window of the bus and wiping their chocolatey fingers on the seat of the bus, between sticking their tongue out at a friend in a silly game and sticking their tongue out at a stranger in the supermarket.

Before you open your mouth to tell your child to do or not do something, ask yourself: does it really matter? Will it harm or upset them or anyone else?

It's already difficult and frustrating enough having so little control over your life when you're a kid. Give them some leeway. Lengthen the leash. Loosen the strings. Allow small freedoms whenever you can!

SIDE-EFFECT
If you're on your child's case all the time, it can come back to haunt you in the way they talk to their siblings and friends: 'Don't do that... That's not allowed... Mummy's going to tell you off for that...' which, in turn, will lead to bickering and squabbles.

9 Set the boundaries

We have just talked about how micromanaging your child can make things worse. But what if you go in the opposite direction? What if you deliberately avoid setting limits because you want to be a kind and relaxed parent, not harsh and strict? Nope, that's not a good idea either!

Research has shown time and time again that if we are too permissive, our children will push and thrash against us until a boundary is reached.

There's got to be a limit somewhere, they think, so they keep going until they hit the edge – even if that's us finally losing our temper and doing something much more drastic than they want, like sending them to their room or taking their toy away.

When you're little, the world is a huge, chaotic and sometimes scary place. You want to make sense of it. You want to know the rules. It makes you feel safe and secure.

Watch a crawling baby, eight or nine months old. Watch him head towards a glass of water on the coffee table. It looks interesting. It looks fun. But he has already learnt from previous experience that it's something he probably shouldn't touch. Watch

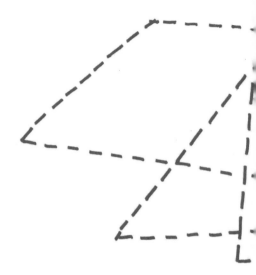

closely as he gets nearer. Notice how just before he gets to the glass, he stops, turns round and looks at his mum. *No!* She warns him gently. *Don't touch that.* He moves a little bit further towards it, stops and looks at her again. Is she going to tell him again? Is she going to move the water? Is she going to pick him up? He could just reach out and touch it but he doesn't because he is testing that there is consistency.

He wants to know that boundary is still there!

When you set limits – as long as they are fair and there for a reason – your child feels reassured. It creates a framework so that instead of challenging you they can get on with enjoying the space and freedom in between the boundaries.

So you don't need to be your child's friend, any more than you need to be your child's boss. Your aim is to be somewhere in the middle. Warm and empathetic, yes, but clear and authoritative at the same time.

Setting a new rule

So you want to fix your four-year-old's bedtime at 7.30pm from now on, or have your nine-year-old tidy their room once a week. Rather than 'Wham bam, this is how it is from now on kid', work WITH your child. Talk to them in advance about what's going to happen and why. Then look for ways to motivate them with positive attention at each step in the right direction. Give them a piggyback when they agree to go up the stairs, sing them a lullaby when they've climbed into bed — even if you'd stopped doing things like that a while ago. Tidy their room with them the first time so you can say, 'Your bookshelf looks great now. What shall we do next?' and finish it off with them the second time even though you know they're perfectly capable of doing it on their own. The new rule is much more likely to stick.

THE BIG PICTURE

Children thrive on consistency but that doesn't mean you need to be 100% rigid and inhuman! If your child is exhausted, maybe you could bend the *put your own pyjamas on* rule tonight. If their baby brother cries all the way through their favourite TV programme, maybe it's okay to tell them they can watch another episode even though you said *only one*.

10 Don't bother with empty threats

> Stop doing that or I'm going to take you home right now.

> If you don't come here, I'm going to go without you.

> If you can't behave, you're not going to Sam's birthday party this afternoon.

Really?!

So you're going to leave your child, go home, put the kettle on and relax? You're going to toss aside the birthday present you've just wrapped up and phone up Sam's mum and explain? You're going to put your coat on and drag your child away this minute?

Nah. You don't believe that and neither do they!

This type of sentence can slip so easily out of our mouths, especially when we're exasperated or feel we've run out of options. But it doesn't take long before your child has heard it all before and realised that you never follow through.

Empty threats are a complete waste of words. They simply don't work. In fact, they undermine your authority.

They give your child the very opposite message to the one you intended.

Your aim was to show your child that you have the power to take things in any direction you want, however drastic. Sam's party starts in under an hour and they've been excited about it all week, but hey, you can still pull the plug on it. But as these threats aren't carried out, they actually give your child the message that you're at a loss. Powerless. They smack of desperation.

The one exception where these types of threats may work – with very young children anyway – is when they refer to a 'higher' authority. For example, *I'll tell daddy when he gets home* or *Right! That's it! I'm going to call the police*, perhaps followed by you starting to make a pretend phone call with your child begging you to stop.

But the reason these work, of course, is only because they frighten your child. Your child co-operates because they are scared of what will happen if they don't. Daddy will tell them off or the police will come *nee-naahing* in their car to get them. But disciplining through fear is neither kind nor helpful. Your aim should be to teach your child that you do something because it is the right or best thing to do, not because of what will happen if they don't. This way they can develop their own inner compass that will guide them to behave appropriately. And anyway, do you really want to present the police to your child as scary people or make daddy the bad guy?!

Speaking with authority

So what's the best way to tell your child to do something? Research shows that your child is most likely to comply if you make a concrete but polite request such as 'Please go and clean your teeth.' This works better than an order ('Go and clean your teeth') or a question ('Will you go and clean your teeth?'). The word 'please' also makes you less likely to use a harsh tone of voice – and it's good role-modelling too! But avoid using it in a pleading ('pleeeeeease') or mock polite, commanding way ('Just do it – PLEASE!') or it'll lose its effectiveness.

Again, these types of threat undermine your authority. It's a kind of admission of your own weakness. *I know I can't control you, but I have access to people who can!*

QUICK TIP
If your child misbehaves when other people such as friends, siblings or relatives are around, they're more likely to do what you say if you say it quietly and close-up to them rather than publicly. No one knows why, but it's true!

11 Don't bribe beforehand – reward afterwards

If you get in the buggy, I'll buy you a packet of crisps.

IIf you finish your homework, I'll give you an extra hour on the computer.

Dangle something before a child's eyes, and – hey presto! – they will often do what you want.

But even if it works, bribery is a bad idea.

When you dish out a bribe, do you actually feel good? In control? Bribes like these are so often given bang in the middle of a difficult situation with your child. In desperation, you find yourself offering them something – anything – just to get them to do what you want.

So rather than putting you in charge, bribes actually put your child in a strong position. They teach them that if they don't co-operate, it may well pay off for them – literally! *Mmm... last time I caused havoc in the supermarket, Mum bought me a chocolate bar to keep me quiet. Maybe I'll try that again.* The bribe can come back to bite you.

It's much better to flip things around.

Notice the good behaviour and reward them for it AFTERWARDS. Swap *If you do that, then this will happen* for *Because you did that, this is going to happen.*

Let's say your child gets dressed all by themself one day and you swoop in with a dinosaur sticker. *Hey, that's awesome!* you say. *I'm going to give you one of these new stickers for that.* Wow! They weren't expecting that! You can FEEL what a powerful effect that would have, can't you? They are much more likely to get dressed by themselves the next day.

The reward doesn't need to be material, like a sticker, a packet of crisps or a cuddly toy. It doesn't need to be an extra hour on the computer or a treat like a trip to the cinema. Remember, what your child most wants is your positive attention so most of the time this will be enough of a reward in itself.

External v. internal motivation

Another reason not to use bribes – or overuse rewards – is that children can become very reliant on them. It becomes a formula in their head: I do this = I get that. The motivation is all external. What we actually want to do is build their own internal motivation so they do things of their own accord. So paying your child money to do household chores may seem like a good idea, for example. It can feel like you're introducing them to 'real life': work = money. But now they're less likely to want to load the dishwasher or clean out the rabbit hutch even though they actually enjoy it or like the feeling that they're helping out. Don't rob them of the opportunity to do something just because it feels good!

Sometimes though, a more tangible reward is useful alongside the positive attention. It can give your child an extra boost for the bigger changes in behaviour. *I'm so pleased you've stayed in your own bed all week,* you might say, *so let's go for a hot chocolate together.*

But make sure you match the size of the reward to the behaviour. If you buy them a magazine for doing something small when a simple *Thanks* would have been enough, you will devalue and desensitise them to those rewards. *Hang on a minute,* they'll be thinking, *you bought me a pony yesterday just for putting my socks on, so…*

QUICK TIP
Be quick to notice behaviours and reward them, especially with very young children. 'I love how you're putting your toys away in the basket, well done!' The immediacy of the reward makes a stronger link in their mind between cause and effect: I did this, so this good thing happened.

12 Reward randomly

Let's talk lab rats for a moment! Lab rat A and lab rat B both live in cages with a lever to press to get pellets of food — but there's a difference. Lab rat A gets a pellet every time he pushes the lever. Lab rat B only sometimes gets a pellet. It can take him one push, three pushes or as many as 13.

What happens? Lab rat A soon loses interest. He only bothers to push the lever when he's hungry. Lab rat B, on the other hand, keeps on pushing that lever whether he's hungry or not. *Maybe this time*, he thinks… *Nope… Maybe this time…or this time…or this time…Yesss!* Every time a pellet comes out, his brain gets a little whoosh of pleasure. It's fun. It's exciting. In fact, he can't stop.

Believe it or not, it's exactly the same with children. Psychologists have known for a very long time that this system of once-in-a-while rewards is the most powerful kind of all.

If your child sees a predictable pattern — *When I do that, this good thing always happens* — it gets

boring. Instead, what you want them to realise is: *When I do that, sometimes this good thing happens and sometimes it doesn't.* That's what'll motivate them to keep repeating that behaviour.

On top of this, if you vary what the actual reward is when it comes, it makes it even more powerful. Think how delighted Lab rat B is going to be if once in a while when he pushes the lever he gets a chunk of cheese or a piece of bacon!

Don't reward your child for a behaviour every time they do it or in the same way. Be unpredictable. Surprise them!

Let's go back to when you swooped in with a dinosaur sticker after your child got dressed by themselves. Imagine if you gave them a sticker the next time too. And the next time. And the next. The effect of it would soon start to wear off, wouldn't it?

But what if the next time you gave them a high five instead? And the next time nothing. And the next time you said, *It's so great that you got dressed by yourself again.* And the next time nothing. And the next time nothing. And the next time a sticker again. You can see how strongly that would spur them on. *When I do that, I just don't know what's going to happen or when,* they'd think sub-consciously. *So I'm going to do it all the time!*

It's not often you'll hear this parenting advice, but when it comes to rewards, be INCONSISTENT!

So what about sticker charts?

Sticker charts go against everything we've just said, right? The reward's always the same (a sticker), it comes every time, and as with a bribe, the child knows beforehand that they're going to get it. Does this make them utterly useless then? Not quite! A sticker chart can help get you 'over a hump' with your child as long as you follow these rules:

1. Only use them very occasionally or they'll lose their impact.
2. Use them for a very specific behaviour, not something general like 'being good'.
3. Use them for a short and defined period of time (e.g. one week). Don't let them just fizzle out.
4. Don't forget to actually give them the sticker!
5. If there's a bigger reward at the end (sometimes the stickers themselves are enough for young children), give it to them as soon as you can — don't leave a big gap.

 QUICK TIP
Never punish your child for a bad behaviour by taking away a reward that you gave them for a good behaviour. That will undo the good it did. It can also make matters worse by making your child feel resentful.

13 Don't randomly reward UNWANTED behaviours

Now here's the booby trap...

While once-in-a-while rewards are great for reinforcing the behaviours we want, they powerfully reinforce behaviours we don't want too – and yet we often reward those behaviours in this way without even realising it!

Scenario 1
Your child pesters you for a fizzy drink from the café every time you go to the swimming pool. Most of the time you refuse. They're expensive and not very healthy. But today, well, you're in a particularly good mood... *Heck, it's only a fizzy drink,* you think and give in and buy them one.

Scenario 2
You're fed up with your child leaving their school uniform all over their bedroom floor when they get undressed in the evening. You start insisting they pick it up. But tonight there's a TV programme you really want to catch at 8pm. It'll be quicker and easier if you pick up their clothes yourself, just this once.

Scenario 3
Your child has discovered the phrase *You big poo-poo* and is using it a lot to provoke a reaction in you. You resolve to totally ignore it from now on until it fizzles out. You manage it for a whole week. Then they say it again just as you've banged your head on the cupboard door. You lose it with them.

Wham! Bang! Wallop! In each case, you've given them a big, fat, once-in-a-while reward for whining, for

How to stop whi-i-i-i-ning

Whining can wind you up like nothing else. So how should you respond? It depends. If your child whines for something you're happy to give them anyway (a piggy-back the rest of the way home?) just prompt them gently with 'Is there a better way you could ask for that?'. But if it's for something you have no intention of giving them (a piggy back all the way home?), respond only to the content of the whine, 'No, I'm sorry, it's too tiring for me to carry you all the way home', and then ignore all further whining. Never show your annoyance or say things like 'Stop whining!' or 'What a horrible voice!'. Giving it attention like that will only encourage it. If however, there's a genuine emotion behind the whine rather than they just turned it on for effect, it will help if you acknowledge that first. 'I can see you really don't feel like walking right now, but...'

leaving their clothes on the floor, for saying those words. Now you've made it much worse.

Let's go back to Lab rat B for a minute. Imagine his lever appears to stop working one day. He pushes it 13, 15, 27 times and still no pellet. *Damn it,* he thinks. *It must be broken.* Then, just at the moment where he is about to give up – on the 34th push – a pellet drops out! *Ohhh!* he thinks, *I was giving up too soon. I just needed to push it more.* And he starts frantically pushing that lever till his little paw is red raw.

Again, it's exactly the same with children. *I just need to whine harder and longer to get a fizzy drink. I'm going to carry on leaving my clothes on the floor because I know she'll pick them up for me eventually. If I say 'You big poo-poo' enough times, I'll get a reaction in the end.*

If, however, you are utterly consistent, the behaviour will dwindle and eventually disappear. They'll give up for good. The whining will stop. They'll pick their clothes up every night. And the words *You big poo-poo* will lose all their interest.

Because no matter how hard I try, they'll think, *I don't get the response I want.*

QUICK TIP

Watch out! Ironically, we are very prone to giving in and rewarding an unwanted behaviour when it has almost disappeared. Why? We are seduced by the improvement in behaviour and get an urge to reward it. 'Oh, okaaay...' you say when they whine for a fizzy drink in a very half-hearted and short-lived way. 'Just today.'

14 Step outside your emotions

In the demanding, day-to-day life of parenting, children can press our buttons so easily – even when they're not doing anything wrong! They only have to innocently fall over and hurt themselves and we can find ourselves snapping, *I TOLD you to be careful* or *That's exactly why you shouldn't run ahead.*

The problem is that these emotionally-fuelled responses are likely to exacerbate the situation.

When our child does something that triggers a negative emotion in us, it will make matters worse if we let that emotion control what we do next.

Let's look at some examples.

Scenario 1
You sit down to dinner. Your child accidentally knocks over their cup of juice. *Oh, for goodness sake – I've only just sat down!* you bark at them. *I didn't do it on purpose,* they say and start pushing their food around their plate sulkily.

Scenario 2
Your child is whinging their way through their homework. You lose your temper and shout at them. Your child bursts into tears and throws their homework across the room.

Scenario 3
Your children are arguing over which TV programme they want to watch. You grab the remote control and say, *Right, I'm turning it off for the rest of the day!* The kids are outraged. They blame each other and start physically fighting.

It is okay and absolutely normal to feel what we feel in these situations. We can't stop ourselves being annoyed, upset or furious – but we can try not to let it interfere and intermingle with our actions.

Here's what can help: when you feel the emotion rising within you, press pause. Take a moment to recognise exactly what you're feeling. Identify it. Label it. Observe the emotion from the outside as if it's separate from you, not within you. Also check in with yourself whether you're already feeling tense about something else entirely (the broken washing machine, an argument with your partner, a hospital appointment tomorrow?) and transferring this to your child. This simple awareness can make it much easier to respond with a cool head.

So yes, the spilt juice is annoying, but maybe now you can say, *It's okay. It was an accident.* Yes, the complaining about the homework is hard to bear, but maybe now you can acknowledge their emotion and say, *I can see you're really not enjoying this homework.* Yes, the arguing over the TV is infuriating, but maybe now you can say, *I'm going to turn the TV off and let you two agree on what to do. Then I'll turn it back on.*

It gets much easier with practice. And even then, you won't always manage it. But every time you do, the situation will be resolved in a faster, fairer and more effective way.

Fake it!

So you feel like screaming, smashing plates and shouting 'You little @~*$%~**!'. Here's a great little trick. After you've taken that moment to focus on what you're feeling, deliberately and artificially speak to your child in a voice that is quiet and gentle – much quieter and gentler than you actually feel! This tricks your brain into thinking you're calm when you're not. It also has a calming rather than a provocative effect on your child.

QUICK TIP

Sometimes, in precisely those moments when you feel the least love, it can help to say to your child, 'I love you very much, but right now I'm really angry'. It reassures and reminds them (and you!) that your anger doesn't change how you feel about them overall. This in itself can help defuse the situation.

15 Give them a choice

Your child is happily playing in the bath. They are well overdue for a hair wash but you know that as soon as you say, *I'm going to have to wash your hair in a minute* – that no matter how gently and nicely you promise to do it – they're going to kick up a huge fuss and it'll end in a big fluster of suds and tears. You're already bracing yourself!

Here's a little trick that can make a big difference.

When you want your child to do something they won't want to do, give your child two options – a choice between two ways of proceeding.

You start (preferably before the bath, to put them in the picture) by saying something like *I'm going to wash your hair tonight.* You also explain why. *We haven't done it for ages. It's quite*

dirty. They need to be clear that it IS going to happen – this bit is not up for negotiation! And then offer a choice. For instance:

Would you like me to do it first and then you can have time to play afterwards or would you like to play first and I'll do it at the end?

Just this tiny amount of choice is often enough to get them on board. As the parent, we make almost all the decisions, leaving them feeling powerless. When you give them a bit of a say in something, it gives them some sense of control and minimises the chance of a battle. Instead of inviting them to clash with you, you're inviting them to co-operate. You're also redirecting their attention from resisting to choosing.

When is a choice not a choice?!

Make sure that the choice you're giving them is a fair and genuine one.
- Both options should be palatable to you – you really don't mind which one they choose.
- Both options should be palatable to them – don't pick one pleasant and one unpleasant one!
- Present both options as equal – don't push them in the direction of one over the other.
- Present both options in a positive, encouraging voice – they're more likely to respond well.
- Don't give choices that just delay the battle, e.g. 'Would you like to go to bed now or stay up for another half an hour?'. They're almost bound to choose to stay up and then you'll still have the same battle 30 minutes later but with a more tired child!
- Never say 'We can do it the easy or the hard way' (i.e. if your child doesn't co-operate, you'll make them do it anyway, kicking and screaming). That's not a choice – it's a threat!

Once you get in the habit, you'll get good at coming up with two options in almost any situation. For example:

Getting into their car seat:
Do you want to climb in yourself or do you want me to lift you in?

Cleaning their teeth:
Shall I squeeze the toothpaste onto the brush or would you like to do it by yourself?

Helping you tidy up toys:
Do you want to pick up the Playmobil® and I'll do the dressing up clothes or the other way round?

Taking medicine you know they don't like:
Would you like strawberry milk or orange juice to take the taste away afterwards?

You decide WHAT is going to happen. They decide HOW it's going to happen.

Be careful not to overuse this technique though. It's exhausting for children if they're continually asked to make choices. Save it for when you sense a sticky situation coming up and then pull it out the bag!

QUICK TIP

You can use this technique with children even before they can talk. Their understanding of language is way ahead of what they can actually say and they'll be able to tell you their preference with gestures or a baby word or two.

16 Tackle one thing at a time – with determination

Last year, these were my New Year's resolutions:

1. Go for a 30-minute speed-walk every morning.
2. Floss my teeth twice a day.
3. Keep a Gratitude Diary.
4. Only watch TV if there's a specific programme I'm interested in.
5. Always take a packed lunch on the train to save money.

How many of these was I still doing at the end of the year? 2¼ out of 5! It was simply too many things for me to change in one go.

It's exactly the same with children.

There may be a whole bunch of things you'd like to change about your child's behaviour but if you try to tackle them all at once you're doomed to failure. Choose the one that feels the most important – and then commit to cracking it!

Suppose you decide to tackle a bedtime problem. Your child keeps getting out of bed in the evening and coming downstairs, asking for a cuddle, a drink of water, a particular toy...

First, choose a week when you're not stressed or extra busy and make a plan of action. A very effective strategy would be to starve this behaviour of attention – to calmly walk your child back to bed without any words or eye contact for as many times as it takes until they stay in bed.

Next, talk to your child. Tell them openly what you want to tackle, why, and how you're going to do it. The more they feel involved, the more chance you have of success.

The three-day rule

It typically takes three days to extinguish or shift a behaviour. Just knowing this can really help you to keep going, however hard it is. This doesn't mean that after three days you'll be done and dusted every time but you're very likely to get to the stage of 'You know, I think we're almost there' or at the very least 'Hang on a minute, things are definitely changing'. This will give you the motivation to see it through to the bitter end. If you really don't see any progress at all after three days, stop, leave a gap, and try a different approach.

Now grit your teeth and go for it!

Expect the first night to be horrible. It may take a 100 times of walking your child back to bed. You'll want to crumble and cave in. *This is too hard,* you'll think. *This is way worse than having an interrupted evening sitting on the sofa.* But stick at it. Be strong. The second night it may still take 50 times and you'll already be exhausted from the first night. You'll waver. You'll wonder if it's worth carrying on. But actually a 50% reduction is really good progress. Keep going. The next night it may only take 10 times… and the next night, *Peeeeeace.*

No pain, no gain! And remember, if you give in at any point, you'll make the situation much worse. Be consistent, persistent and resistant.

And sometimes, just sometimes, the process may not be anywhere near as bad as you're bracing yourself for. Take this case of a mother who talked to her four-year-old daughter about giving up the training beaker she was very attached to. The plan was to systematically reduce how often she had her drink in it over two weeks. Day one: The girl simply picked up the cup and put it in the bin!

QUICK TIP
When your child reluctantly does something you've asked them to do, completely ignore any 'add-on' behaviours like moaning, sulking or huffing and puffing. If they stamp their feet loudly on the stairs as they go off to brush their hair, they're still brushing their hair. Give all your attention to the positive ('You've done a good job!'), not the negative ('There's no need to stamp your feet like that!')

17 Don't be wordy

There's a tendency to think that when we instruct or reprimand our child, the more we expand and elaborate, the more they will take notice of us and do what we say. Rather than saying, *Can you go upstairs and get your dirty school uniform please,* words can come tumbling out of our mouth:

Go upstairs and get your dirty school uniform please because if I don't put a wash on now it won't be dry by tomorrow and then you'll have to wear the cardigan you say is all itchy and you hate wearing that. Go on, go and get it. It's on your bed, I think. The one you were wearing yesterday. I need to put a wash on now.

But repetition, long-windedness and going off at tangents makes what we have to say less, not more, powerful.

Fewer words have a greater impact. Your child is more likely to listen to you and do what you say if you are brief and to the point.

Children will only listen for a certain length of time before they zone you out. In fact, if you frequently ramble on or lecture them, they will learn to stop listening to you the moment you start speaking. Alternatively, they'll try to 'escape' the torrent of words by arguing back or doing something else you don't like to create a distraction. You have much more chance of them going along with you – even if it's only with a reluctant *Okaaay* – when you keep what you have to say short and succinct.

 QUICK TIP
When you're busy or stressed, you may find yourself bombarding your child with a list of instructions in order to 'empty out' your own head: 'When you've learnt your spellings, I want you to get me your lunchbox out your bag, give these carrots to the guinea pigs and then come and write nanny's birthday card'. Don't! It's overwhelming for them and you'll almost certainly have to repeat some or all of it.

It's particularly easy to fall into lecturing mode if your child does something that presses one of your buttons. Perhaps your child told you a lie and you spotted it. Whoosh! You're off on one! You need them to understand why lying is so wrong and you're going to keep going... and going... until they get it. But they won't because they already stopped listening five sentences ago. Your message will be much stronger if you keep it bite-sized: *It's important you tell me the truth because it breaks the trust between you and me when you don't.* And stop. Right. There. If you carry on, it'll just disintegrate into *blah blah blah* to your child and undermine the message you have already clearly given.

If you feel there really is more to say on the topic, raise it calmly and gently at another time, not now when things are tense and prickly. Most of the time there really will be no need.

No need to shout!

When we shout at our child, they may comply, but only because shouting is scary and intimidating – or at the very least annoying – and they want it to stop. It doesn't lead to any real behaviour change. Firstly, children are very sensitive to tone of voice and when you use a loud and forceful voice, they feel stressed and tune into the emotion of what you're saying, not the content. The message is mostly lost. Secondly, shouting is bad role-modelling and encourages your child to shout back at you and others. Of course, we will all sometimes end up shouting at our child (let's be realistic!) but the less we do it, the better.

18 Make routine your friend

Some of you may baulk at the word 'routine'. It may bring images of matronly nannies with starched aprons and chest watches into your head! *Where's the room for spontaneity? you cry!*

But research shows that in families where there is a feeling of structure and predictability, rather than a feeling that you're just muddling through, children behave better.

This absolutely doesn't mean you need to routinise each and every moment of your child's daily life. Not at all. Focus on the hot spots – the bits of your day or week where you find yourself nagging your child and getting into arguments over the same old list of things. *Hurry up and get dressed... No, you need to have breakfast first... Have you got your water bottle?* It might be getting out the house on a school morning, getting ready for bed, or leaving for gymnastics on a Saturday.

When you systemise and streamline day-to-day tasks, your child knows what to expect and what is expected – and accepts it. You won't have to badger them and get into battles. They'll operate on autopilot.

You can stop being the bad guy. Because the routine, rather than you, will dictate what happens. Everyone will know, for example, that bedtime begins at 7.30 and unfolds like this:

1. Feed and say goodnight to the hamster.
2. Go to the bathroom to clean teeth and go to the toilet.
3. Get changed into pyjamas in bedroom.
4. Put school uniform on chair ready for the next day.
5. Choose two picture books from the shelf.
6. Listen to the books while they drink their milk.
7. Lights out.

It's just what happens at this time of day, they'll think.

What's more, children like learning to do things for themselves without reminders. It makes them feel competent and independent – *I'm in charge of myself!* – so they have even less reason to dig their heels in or put up a fight.

There's no need for these mini-routines to restrict your life or make you a slave to the clock. They simply mean that certain things happen in a certain way and in a certain order. You want to stay up late to watch the fireworks? You're going to stay over with relatives for a family party? Or maybe you're just having such fun playing *Dobble*™ that you overshoot their normal bedtime? No worries. As long as they know the drill, whatever time it is, and wherever you are, they can jump into action.

Training their brain

The part of the brain responsible for planning ahead, the pre-frontal cortex, isn't fully formed until around age 25. This means children are easily lost in the moment. They were meant to be feeding the fish and they've got distracted by the hamster! You sent them upstairs for their jumper and they've come down with a Rubik's™ cube! When you're setting up a new routine, look for ways to help them stay on task. You could draw step-by-step pictures of the things they need to do on a school morning and put them on the front door. You could nudge them along with visual clues: lay their clothes out on the sofa, squeeze the toothpaste onto their toothbrush and put their shoes on the doormat. You could tell them there are five things to do – two upstairs and three downstairs – and then if they get lost after three, at least they'll know there are two more and have a chance of recalling them.

SIDE-EFFECT

Rituals and repetition also create more opportunity for moments of cosiness and connection. Instead of using your time and energy to move your child on from one task to another, you might have a snuggle in bed when they first wake up or do a silly dance with them while they're cleaning their teeth.

19 Make up and move on

Just a few minutes ago, your child did something that made your blood boil. Now, just a few minutes later, they're chirpy and cheerful. *Mummy, look what the ducks are doing!* they're saying. *You little so-and-so,* you think. You don't respond. You want them to know that they may have forgotten all about it but you most definitely have not!

Children bounce back very quickly. You can often see their mood change before your eyes. Adults, by contrast, often hold on tight to their negative emotions. *I'm having a bad day,* we say to ourselves, *and on that day my mood is going to be black*! But if you give your child the cold shoulder, they're much more likely to do something else to provoke you to get you to re-engage with them – and then you're in a vicious circle. It's really important to try to bounce back with them.

Re-attune and reconnect with your child as quickly as possible after they've done something that angered or upset you.

Of course, it's not easy to do when your blood is still simmering! But research shows that even a fake smile lowers your heart rate and helps you to recover more quickly from a stressful situation. So if you force yourself to soften your face and say, *Oh yes, the ducks are upside*

down dipping their heads in the water! you really will start to feel better.

Be ready and willing to admit your mistakes too. If you feel you reacted too harshly or unfairly to what they did, apologise as soon as possible. Saying *I'm sorry I yelled at you* or *I'm*

sorry I grabbed the hairbrush off you like that isn't a sign of weakness. It won't make their behaviour worse. Quite the opposite. Apologising to your child is great role-modelling. It shows them you're a human being who sometimes messes up, and that's okay, as long as you're willing to acknowledge it. You'd want them to be able to say to their friend, *I know I said I'd never play with you again but I didn't mean it – sorry*, wouldn't you?

In every case, the sooner you come back with some warmth and positivity, the sooner you'll be back on track to have a harmonious time together.

'Say sorry!'

After our child has done something wrong, often our instinctive reaction is to make them apologise – to us, their sibling or whoever was affected. Don't! Forcing an apology teaches them that the word 'sorry' is a quick fix – whether they feel sorry or not. What we want is to develop their genuine empathy and compassion. If they can put themselves in someone else's shoes, they are much less likely to repeat the behaviour. Instead, turn all your attention to the victim, not your child. Comfort them and say, 'I'm really sorry' on their behalf. Later, when things are calm, talk to your child about how their behaviour made the other person (or you) feel.

QUICK TIP

If, on the other hand, your child apologises of their own accord, accept it whole-heartedly and graciously. Don't prolong or re-ignite the issue by saying 'Well, it's just not good enough' or 'Why do you always do that?'.

20 Let **THEM** come up with a solution

Sometimes the same battle with your child comes up again and again. Let's say they keep getting up and down from the table during family meals and it's driving you nuts. *I need the toilet, I'm just going to put my socks on, I want to get a different spoon...* they say.

You've tried everything from ignoring it entirely to a sticker chart, but nothing's worked. So now what?

A technique that can be very effective with a persistent problem is to ask your child what THEM think will help them change their behaviour. Put THEM in charge of solving the problem.

Choose a time and place separate from the 'scene of the crime', when you're both feeling relaxed and happy with each other. (Never use this technique in the heat of the moment or you'll just get back into a battle.) You could take them for a walk, for example, or sit in the park with a flask of hot chocolate.

Then raise the issue gently and uncritically. Talk about it objectively as if it's a 'thing' you are examining – a problem to be solved, not something personal. *You seem to be having a hard time staying at the dinner table. It spoils mealtimes and I get cross – it's not very nice for either of us, is it? I'm wondering*

A drastic example... that worked!

A mum had to nag her eight-year-old daughter to get ready for school every single morning. 'Haven't you even cleaned your teeth yet?...Go and get your book bag...you haven't got time to play with that now'. One Saturday afternoon, the mum invited her daughter to sit opposite ends of the sofa, face to face, under a blanket, and brainstorm what she thought might help. The daughter was crystal clear. 'I want you to tell me what time we have to leave – only that – and then if I'm not ready, I want you to walk out the door without me.' The mum (secretly!) flinched. That sounded super-risky but she agreed to do it. From then on her daughter was ready on time. Yes, she sometimes scrabbled to get ready at the last minute, but she always made it.

what we can do about it. The ideas I've come up with don't seem to be helping. Have YOU got any good ideas? What do you think would help you to stay at the table?

Children will often come up with all sorts of weird and wonderful 'solutions' – things we as adults would never think of! *I'd stay at the table if me and daddy swapped places* or *I want to have a glass of water with a slice of lemon in it at dinner time.*

Huh! Like that'll work! you might think. But no matter how ridiculous or off-the-wall their 'solutions' sound to you, listen and accept their suggestions without judgement or negative comments. As long as they make sense to them, that's all that matters.

Keep talking until they've hit upon an idea they really like – and one that is also fine by you too (*I'd like to have my pudding first* may not cut it!) – and

agree to put it into action the next time the problem comes up.

This way, rather than imposing a solution on them, you are giving them ownership of it. They feel involved, listened to, respected and above all, responsible for whether it works or not. It's as if they're entering into a contract with you. *It was my idea,* they think, *so I'd better make it work!*

21 Don't give them labels or expectations to live up to

She was born naughty!

I want you to be a good boy for grandma.

A mother was choosing nappies in a chemist and jiggling her newborn baby in the pram to try to stop her grizzling. After a couple of minutes, she picked her up and she quietened down. *You naughty little thing,* she said affectionately, kissing her baby's head. *I can't pick you up every two minutes, you know. You need to be a good girl for mummy and stay in your pram.*

See how soon and how easily words like *naughty* and *good* creep in. This mum is still oozing with love for her newborn and the baby doesn't yet have a clue what she's saying – but those words are there already!

Beware! This is a bad habit to slip into.

Children tend to take on and live up to labels and expectations. Calling them things like 'naughty' or 'nothing but trouble' can only make their behaviour worse. Even telling them to 'be good' or 'behave yourself' shows them you expect them not to.

People keep calling me naughty, thinks the child who is often called naughty. *So I guess it's just the way I am. Nothing I can do about it.* Equally the child labelled *good* or *easy* will feel pressure to behave in a certain and perhaps unnatural way. We humans are a complicated mixture of genes and environment and it's certainly possible to have a child who is more difficult or easier than another, but pigeonholing them will only exacerbate the difference – and breed jealousy and resentment between siblings.

Although it's more subtle, it works in the same way when we tell our child how we want them to behave. *Be a good girl,* we might say as we drop them off at a birthday party or play date, or *If I take you swimming I don't want any messing about in the changing rooms like last time, okay?* This sets you up for trouble. The message your child receives is that you're already thinking badly of them. *She's not expecting me to behave well... So why bother?* Now you actually have less, not more, chance of them behaving well than if you'd said nothing at all.

The Naughty Step

Putting your child on the 'naughty step' or in 'time out' (much better term – lost that N word!) for a minute per year of their age is a commonly used technique. But is it a good idea? Here's what research shows:

• 'Time in' (giving your child periods of focused attention) is a much more powerful way to improve their behaviour.

• It's very effective with some children and not at all with others. If your child just sits and sings to themselves or works themselves up into a rage, stop using it.

• Longer is not better. Whatever their age, don't make it longer than five minutes.

• It's best saved for extreme behaviours like aggression or destruction. It gives your child (and you) a chance to cool off.

• It loses its effectiveness if you shout, lecture or argue with them. Just say simply and calmly why you're giving them time out, e.g. 'You hit me and that's not okay'.

• It loses its effectiveness if you forget the time. Setting a timer is a good idea. It depersonalises the situation and stops the child constantly asking 'Is the time up yet?'.

So keep shtum. Then afterwards, if they do behave well, get out your magic wand and sprinkle them with some praise and positive attention!

QUICK TIP

Don't put ideas in your child's head! If I say to you 'Don't think of an orange unicorn with three legs', what happens? Your brain automatically forms an image of an orange unicorn with three legs. Similarly, if you say to your child 'I don't want you flicking your peas today' as you give them their dinner, they will immediately picture pea flicking and are more, not less, likely to do it!

22 Use consequences, not punishments

From a good telling-off to sending them to bed early to stopping their pocket money, parents have been punishing children since time began. The aim? To teach them a lesson.

Yet that's exactly what punishments don't do!

Yes, your child may comply – but only because the punishment is unpleasant. Once the punishment is lifted or you're not around, the same behaviour is likely to crop up again.

Here's why.

Firstly, punishments shift the focus onto you, not the behaviour. *I hate you!* or *That's so unfair* they feel (or scream!), not *I made a mistake* or *I won't do that next time*. Instead of thinking about what they've done wrong, they fixate on their anger or resentment.

Secondly, punishments don't teach your child how to behave in a better way. All they learn is that it's okay to be mean to someone if they do something you don't like. They may even retaliate or lie to you to try to dodge the punishment.

 QUICK TIP
Never make the consequence something you want them to like, e.g. 'If you don't turn the Xbox off now so we have time to do your reading, you'll have no Xbox at all tomorrow and we'll do reading instead'.

Consequences, by contrast, work in a very different way. They focus on the behaviour and flow logically from what the child has done wrong. Let's look at an example for comparison:

Your child has drawn on the wall with their felt-tip pens.

Punishment approach: You yell *That's really naughty! Go to your room and stay there until I tell you to come out. I'm not taking you to the park now.*
Child thinks: *Urgggh!* They stomp off and start kicking the wall in their bedroom.

Consequence approach: You say matter-of-factly, *That's really spoilt the look of the wall. I'm going to have to try and clean it off now so we'll have less time to spend in the park.*
Child thinks: *Mmmm, I can see that it is quite a bit of work. Fair enough, I suppose.*

Consequences allow your child to directly experience the effects of their actions so they can make a better choice in the future. Let's look at some more examples.

Your child breaks their brother's toy in anger.
Consequence: They have to use their pocket money to buy another one for their brother.

Your child lies to you about not having homework.
Consequence: You say you'll have to check with their teacher every week until you trust they're telling you the truth again.

Your 10-year-old keeps leaving their dirty clothes on their bedroom floor.
Consequence: You say you're only going to wash clothes put in the dirty laundry basket (next time she wants to wear a particular T-shirt it's screwed up and dirty).

A consequence is purely about the facts of what happened. So rather than a personal war, consequences operate more like a business agreement!

Put your thinking cap on

Sometimes it takes a bit of thought and creativity to come up with a good consequence. It's okay to tell your child you'll get back to them and think it through. Ask yourself: 'What does my child need to learn?' and 'What would be the most effective way to teach that?'. It can help to sit down and write yourself a 'menu' of consequences for the most common situations so they're ready to use when you need one. And sometimes the natural consequence of what they've done wrong will be enough. For example, if they didn't stay close to you in the shop as you asked and they got lost and upset, that's a learning experience in itself.

23 Don't forget they're watching you!

Have you ever seen a one-year-old pick up a phone and start babbling into it? Or a two-year-old give his teddy a good telling-off? Or a three-year-old rub the pointy end of a strawberry on her lips as if she's putting on lipstick?

No one taught them to do that. They're simply imitating what they've seen their parents do.

Your behaviour is contagious. It has a direct and incredibly powerful effect on your child's behaviour. Don't underestimate it!

In the early years, especially before they go to school, your child is absolutely tuned in to watch and copy your behaviour. It's how nature designed them so that they learn the skills they need to survive and thrive. The problem is that so often they see us do things we don't want them to copy. It's one rule for them and one rule for us.

Don't shout at me! we might shout at them or *It's not nice to snatch!* as we snatch a toy off them that they took from another child. *You silly little boy,* we might say even though we tell them off when they call people names, or *Don't say horrible things about Auntie Jenny* despite the fact that they've heard us criticising Auntie Jenny behind her back all the time.

When you model a behaviour, you give your child a very strong message: this behaviour is appropriate and acceptable. *Mummy or Daddy does it... so it must be okay,* they think. Sooner or later, that behaviour will be reflected back at you!

It's really important to step back from time to time and ask yourself:

Am I behaving in a way I would be happy for my child to copy? Also, be honest with yourself about whether any of their behaviours that you don't like originated from you. The connection is not always immediately obvious.

Suppose you're watching TV and your child asks to watch something else and you say, *Nope. I'm watching this, so tough!* Is that what you'd want them to say to their brother? Or would you rather they said something kinder, like, *This is my favourite programme. Let me finish watching it and you can choose the next programme.*

Perhaps your child picks up a pair of scissors and you swipe them away without any explanation. Then it wouldn't be altogether surprising if they swiped a Lego® brick off another child. But if instead you take the scissors and say, *They're really sharp – you might hurt yourself,* then you're more likely to hear them say something softer to the other child, like, *I really need that brick for my roof.*

Of course, none of us can be a perfect role model all day every day but as long as you're willing to admit your imperfections – *I know you heard me say that to the traffic warden but it wasn't nice and I shouldn't have said it* – the damage will be limited!

QUICK TIP

Think out loud! If you share your thought processes with your child, they can learn even more from you. Say to them on the bus, 'That man looks like he's got a bad leg, so I'm going to be kind and offer him my seat', or as you're getting ready for a party, 'I'm feeling really nervous because I won't know anyone there but I'm just going to dive in and talk to people'.

Smacking: The facts

Smacking a child role models that when you're angry or unhappy with what somebody's done, it's okay to hit them. Some parents argue, 'It didn't do me any harm as a kid' or 'A short, sharp shock works better than anything else' but hundreds of studies have been done on smacking and not a single one of them shows it's a good idea! It may 'work' at the time – but only because the child fears another smack. The effect is temporary. Long-term, children who are smacked are more, not less, likely to misbehave. They're also more likely to lie and be secretive to avoid a smack and to be aggressive to their siblings, peers, you – and later in life to their own children and partners.

24 Minimise hunger and tiredness

Tiredness or hunger = trouble. They bring out the worst in all of us, but for children who are still learning to regulate their emotions, they can bring out the 'Incredible Hulk'!

It's easy to assume your child is deliberately misbehaving when they are actually tired or hungry. If you manage their tiredness and hunger levels, their behaviour will be easier to manage too.

The first thing of course (basic as it is!) is to feed and water them at regular intervals. It doesn't have to be clockwork – 12.55 rather than 12.30 on the dot for lunch isn't a problem. But if breakfast, lunch and dinner come at roughly the same time every day, especially when children are very young, it helps to keep blood sugar levels and behaviour on a more even keel. In between meals, you may worry that snacks will 'spoil' their lunch or dinner, but you don't want to leave them to get so hungry that things kick off! Swooping in with a healthy snack mid-morning and mid-afternoon will prevent this and still leave plenty of time for them to be the right amount of hungry by mealtime.

'How much out of 10?'

A useful question to ask your child, especially when you're out and about and want to decide when to stop and eat, is 'How hungry are you out of 10?' (Where 0 = not at all and 10 = ravenous!). It works for the toilet too. 'How much do you need to go out of 10?' you can ask on a long car journey, for example. Then you know whether it can wait until the next service station (7 out of 10) or if you really do need to pull up at the nearest bush (9½ out of 10!). As long as your child sees that you always respond appropriately, they'll give you an honest answer without wild exaggeration.

Similarly, a regular bedtime that is appropriate for the age of your child, plus naps for younger children, will help enormously. There will of course still be days when they get less sleep than they need (they had a sleepover... they were lying awake worrying about something...) but just accept that they are likely to be out of sorts the following day and don't make demands of them which are unrealistic. If you'd been to a party until three in the morning, you probably wouldn't choose to go on a 30-mile cycle ride or re-tile the whole bathroom the following day!

Watch out too for those sentences that slip out so easily, like, *You're really tired – you went to bed way too late last night* or *The problem is you're hungry – you should have eaten all your breakfast like I told you to.* Not only do these rebukes sound like you're blaming them (and even if it is their fault, telling them why they're grumpy will only make them grumpier!), they also squash their emotions. It may be obvious to you that their extreme frustration when they get in a twist and tangle putting on their tights one Sunday morning is caused or exacerbated by tiredness, but their frustration is still real! It will ease the situation more quickly if you acknowledge their emotion before offering perhaps a lie-down on the sofa with a film.

THE BIG PICTURE

Your child may not be able to tell you they're hungry or tired – because they may not know themselves. As adults, we can recognise when tiredness or hunger is making us feel grumpy. We know we need to grab a banana or have an early night. But in young children, the bit of the brain that makes that link isn't fully developed yet.

25 Beware of boredom

A mother was with her four-year-old son in a doctor's waiting room… waiting… and waiting… and waiting. The boy had already played with the activity cube in the corner and got his mum to read the few picture books on the shelf. Now, 50 minutes later, he was rolling on the floor and sliding the magazines off the table one by one. *Stop doing that!* she said. *Will you just behave?*

Was he actually misbehaving? No. He was beside himself with boredom.

The thing about being a kid is you have to hang out with a grown-up a lot of the time in grown-up situations which hold no stimulation for you: a long, slow queue in the post office, a 'big shop' at the supermarket, your mum stopping to chat with someone in the street for *aaaaages…*

Don't expect your child to have the patience of an adult. If you're in a situation which is tedious for them, find a way to alleviate their boredom. Otherwise they may look to amuse themselves in ways you don't like.

When you can predict they're going to get bored, come prepared. For example, an audio book to break up a three-hour car journey could be a lifesaver. One of those cardboard 'magic' drawing slates might be just the thing to keep them entertained during an older sibling's hour-long recorder concert. Putting a piece of wool in your pocket would mean you could play cat's cradle with them while you're waiting to see the optician.

When you get caught unexpectedly in a boring situation, improvise! Show them how to make a paper aeroplane out of a flu-jab leaflet when you're waiting to be seen at the Minor Injuries unit, for instance. Set them the challenge of seeing how many animals they can spot in a *Good Housekeeping* magazine while the hairdresser finishes your (very slow!) haircut. Play noughts and crosses on a serviette during a ridiculously long wait for your food in a café.

Cat's cradle? Noughts and crosses? you may be thinking. *Get with it grandma! I've got a smartphone in my bag.*

True, a phone or tablet is a portable and easy way to amuse your child in any situation but a dependence on it will make your life harder, not easier. Take this case of a father in a clothes shop, struggling to rifle through the piles of jeans and manoeuvre his two-year-old in a pushchair – while also holding an iPad® playing a CBeebies video in front of her face at the same time! Whenever the screen moved out of the child's vision, even for a moment, she complained loudly. Once you've used a screen to entertain your child it can become a battleground if you try to say *No* after that. Rather than reaching for it automatically, try to use technology as a last resort.

ROOM.

QUICK TIP

Never play all your cards at once. Don't board the train from London to Glasgow and immediately unpack everything you've brought to entertain them and say, 'Look! This lot should keep you going for five hours!'. Let them settle in, gaze out the window, chat, make up their own games... Then, when you see the restlessness really kick in, start drip-feeding them some entertainment, one thing at a time.

26 Take it step-by-step

When your child does something you don't like, it's easy to go from 0-100 mph in 10 seconds and pounce on anything that comes into your head. *If you leave your bike out on the driveway one more time I'm going to lock it in the shed for the rest of the holidays!*

Uh oh! Now what? You've backed yourself into a corner.

Avoid jumping straight to the 'end point'. Move gradually and gently, step by step, through a series of strategies so that your child has the chance to stop, think, learn and make a better choice at any stage.

Every situation will be different – there's no set formula – but let's look at two examples of how this might work.

Example 1
Your two-year-old is shaking their trainer cup of milk all over the kitchen floor.

Step 1: Pause. Step outside of your emotions.

Step 2: Ask yourself: *Is this purely for attention?* If so, ignore it. If it doesn't stop, go to Step 4.

Step 3: Calmly tell them to stop and explain why, e.g. makes a mess, is extra work for you.

Step 4: Try to redirect their attention (*Let's go to the living room and do that jigsaw puzzle*) whilst asking yourself: *Are they hungry, tired or bored? Do they need their attention levels topped up?* If they still don't stop…

Step 5: Think of a consequence and calmly give a warning. *If you keep doing that, I'm going to have to put you in your high chair so that I can clean the floor.* If they still don't stop…

Step 6: Give one last warning. If they still don't stop…

Step 7: Put them gently and calmly in their high chair without saying anything. Ignore 'add-on' behaviours like protests or pushing you away.

Step 8: Clear up the floor. Maybe pop a toy on their high chair (remember you're not trying to punish them).

Step 9: Take them out of their high chair and reattune and reconnect with them quickly, e.g. *Let's go to the living room and do that puzzle now.*

Undo the damage

When you do dish out an out-of-proportion punishment, the best thing to do is retract it. This won't undermine your authority as long as you do it openly and directly. 'I know I said I'd lock your bike in the shed for the rest of the holidays, but I overreacted...' and then give them a fairer consequence. Don't just wait until the next time they ask if they can go on their bike and say passively 'Oh...alright then'. That WILL undermine your authority!

QUICK TIP

When they're very little, it's easy to physically control your child: put them in the highchair, take something off them, carry them out of the park when they don't want to leave – but you're going to struggle to do that when they're bigger!

If you get into the habit of telling them what you're going to do before they can walk or talk – 'Daddy's going to put you in the buggy now' – it sets up a healthier and more respectful dynamic.

Example 2

You discover at 10.30 pm that your nine-year-old has secretly taken the iPad® to bed.

Step 1: Pause... you know the rest!

Step 2: Calmly and briefly explain to them why this not a good thing to do e.g. It makes them tired the next day, it breaks your trust.

Step 3: Ask them to hand over the iPad®.

Four days later, you catch them at it again. Repeat steps 1-3 and:

Step 4: Give them a consequence. *From now on I want you to hand the iPad® to me at bedtime.*

A week later it happens again (you'd got a bit lax about them handing it over!). Repeat Steps 1-3 and:

Step 5: Let them come up with a solution. *Can you think of how you could stop yourself being tempted to do this again?* Put their solution into action.

Three weeks later, there they are AGAIN!

Step 6: Give them a warning of a bigger consequence. *If it happens again, I'm going to take the iPad away completely for a week.*

Step 7: If it happens again, carry out the consequence.

27 Tackle technology

Is it a monster that eats children's brains? Or is it a wonderful tool that enriches their lives? Whatever your thoughts on technology, one thing's for sure, unpeeling a child from a screen isn't easy!

Screens can suck you in and make you lose track of everything else. So you may find yourself tussling with a child who not only doesn't want to stop, but is also hungry and needs the loo!

How do we minimise these battles?

The first thing is to decide precisely what limits you want to put in place. It might be 20 minutes screen-time a day or 20 hours a week to spread out or binge on as they wish. You might stipulate no technology before breakfast or after 6pm, or that it's not allowed at the dinner table or when friends are over to play. As long as everyone is clear about the rules, they'll be much easier to enforce. If you make them up as you go along – *Come on, turn it off now. You've been on it all morning!* – you'll come up against a lot more resistance.

Then find ways to depersonalise the limits you've set. Making a chart to put on the wall that everyone can see and no-one can argue with is a good idea. Your child can cross off or fill in their time allowance as they use it up. Setting a timer is also really useful and stops you having to keep an eye on the clock or be the baddie who announces *Time's up!*

Now be sure to stick to those limits. Be consistent. If you sometimes give in to whining or pleading – *Oh, I suppose another half hour won't hurt,*

Screen-free days

Huge numbers of studies are being done into the effects of technology on children, but it's still a relatively new area. But we don't need the results of research to know that the more time a child spends on a screen, the less time they spend squidging plasticine or swinging on the monkey bars in the park or dressing up and making a show with their friend – and children need these types of experiences too to develop and thrive. Building screen-free days (or even a whole week!) into your family life will reduce their pull towards technology. Present it more as a challenge than a ban. For example, 'We're going to have one day this weekend where none of us go on a screen!'. Then use the time to do other fun things together and give them some focused attention. They may complain and pine for technology at first, but you (and your child!) might be surprised at how happy they are off-screen.

just today – you'll make it a lot worse for yourself. (Remember that lab rat and his little worn-out paw?!)

That doesn't mean being rigid to the second. If you were reading a book, you'd hate it if someone said *Stop RIGHT NOW* in the middle of a sentence or an exciting part, wouldn't you? *I just want to finish this bit,* you'd say. If you're sensitive to them in the same way with technology, it will avoid unnecessary battles.

Sometimes it will be tempting to let your child go over their limit because a friend has come round for a chat, for example, or you need to secretly do some online Christmas shopping. That's fine – as long as you're upfront about it. Tell them you're giving them 'bonus' or 'extra' screen time and why. If you just let it happen without saying anything, you'll be storing up trouble for next time. *Ohhh, but yesterday we got longer! Why can't we now?*

Finally, when battles do arise, take it step by step from warning to consequence. What's the most logical consequence in this case? Loss of screen-time of course!

THE BIG PICTURE
Remember, your behaviour is contagious. If you're on a screen a lot, your child will want or expect to be on a screen a lot too. It looks no different to them if you're on social media or doing an online food shop. So when you're doing something necessary or constructive, show them that.

28 Don't dive into sibling squabbles

On average, siblings have a conflict about once every 18 minutes, lasting on average around a minute. But do you know what else?

Siblings fight around TWICE as much when a parent's there! Yep, we (accidentally!) make it worse.

Let's say you hear your children fighting over a little ride-on plastic car in the garden. Your instinct is to jump in and put an end to it quickly. *Let your little brother go on it for five minutes and then swap over.* That seems fair. Sorted, right? Probably not! Your 'solution' can cause more problems than it solves.

What seems fair to you may feel outrageously unfair to them. *But he went on the car first last time,* whines one. *But it was MY birthday present!* snarls the other. You have simply added fuel to the fire.

So what should you do instead? Butt out!

When you hear an argument break out, do absolutely nothing at first. Hold back and see if they resolve it

quickly themselves. If they don't, or if they come complaining about each other to you, say:

This sounds like something I think you two can sort out between you. I'm going to give you a few minutes to see if you can.

And leave them to it again.

Things may escalate at first, but hold your nerve. When you show trust and confidence in their ability to sort it out themselves, it makes them believe they can. It doesn't matter what solution they come up with – perhaps they decide to squash onto the car together or turn it upside down and use the wheels as steering wheels – as long as it works for them.

If after a few minutes, however, they still haven't reached a solution, ask *Do you need me to help you a bit?* If you didn't witness what happened, remind them *I wasn't there so I don't know what happened.* This makes it clear that you're not going to have assumptions about who did what. Then listen evenly to both sides, without making any judgement about who is right and wrong – and then still pass it back over to them! *Hmmm... so what do you think would be the best thing to do?* Now gently guide them towards some possible solutions.

It may sound labour-intensive, but it will soon pay off. When children are allowed a bit of time and space to come up with their own solutions, they get better and better at it. With time, the frequency, ferocity and length of their arguments will reduce – and they will come running to you a lot less!

QUICK TIP

When your children are having a conflict, always ask yourself if there are any contributing factors like tiredness, hunger or boredom. Is it time for the younger one's nap? Do they need a snack? Do they need an attention top-up?

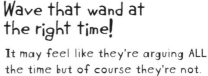

Wave that wand at the right time!

It may feel like they're arguing ALL the time but of course they're not. Catch them when they're NOT arguing and pounce with some positive attention. Pop your head in and say, 'That game sounds like fun' or 'You two are playing so well together'. On the flip side, don't let them hear (or overhear!) you saying how they much they fight. Comments like 'Why can't you two just get along?' or 'I'm so fed up of them fighting' give them attention for it – as well as an expectation to live up to!

29 Don't take sides

Six-year-old Cara has her best friend round to play. They're in her bedroom having a lot of fun building a den — except that her four-year-old brother keeps barging into the room.

She stomps downstairs. *Mummy, Eddie won't leave us alone. He's spoiling our game!* she complains. *Come on, he's only little, he just wants to join in,* replies her mum. *Why does she always stick up for him just because he's younger?* thinks Cara, stomping back upstairs. *Go away!* she screams at Eddie and slams the door in his face. Eddie starts wailing. *Muuuuummy!*

Oh boy! Here we go...

It's so easy to favour one child over the other — sometimes without even realising it. But not only will this inflame the immediate situation, if it keeps happening, it will also inject a deeper-rooted resentment and antagonism into their feelings towards their sibling — and you! This will foster more arguments and make them come running to you more often if they think they can use your bias to their advantage.

Often our tendency is to look out for the younger child but not always. The mum (especially if she was a first-born herself) might have responded, *Eddie, it's her bedroom and her friend. They need some big-girl time on their own.* Then Eddie would have felt the resentment. *Why does she always take Cara's side just because she's older? I never get to do anything!* He might even have gone into Cara's room and destroyed their den.

With siblings, you should aim to be on neither side and both sides at the same time. How do you do that?! It's a trick we've learnt already: simply acknowledge what they're feeling.

I can see that's really annoying for you... you want some time to play on your own with your friend, the mum could say to Cara. *I can see you feel really left out... you'd really like to be able to join in with them,* the mum could say to Eddie. *Would you like to help me make lunch instead?* she might add.

It's important to accept and allow siblings to express their negative feelings towards each other. When they feel heard and understood, it really can defuse the situation very quickly.

I HATE him! sobbed a girl after an argument with her younger brother. *I wish he'd never been born. I want him to go and live with another family!*

The mum's instinct was to reply *You mustn't say horrible things like that. He's your brother and you love him really.*

But instead she said, *I can see you're feeling really angry with him… it's really difficult for you to have a little brother sometimes.* The girl took a big sniff and immediately bounced off to play with her brother again!

Same is not equal

You buy a book for one child, so you feel you should buy one for the other. You let one child have a friend for a sleepover, so you invite a friend for the other one too. You take them to the funfair and allow each child three rides at £2 each. That way, you think, there'll be no arguments or complaints of 'It's not fair!'. But each of your children is unique with different likes, interests and needs. Maybe the other child would much prefer a bouncy ball to a book. Maybe the other child loves their sleep and hates the idea of a sleepover. Maybe one child really just wants one go on the big wheel (£5). It actually creates more contentment and harmony when you recognise and treat your children as individuals.

QUICK TIP

When a new baby arrives, an older sibling often feels pushed out and acts up. Having someone else take care of the baby so you can give the older child some focused, one-to-one attention – even for a short time – can make a big difference.

30 Look after yourself

We may harbour the notion that we should be relishing every precious moment with our offspring as we blow raspberries on their tummy and bake teddy-bear-shaped biscuits with them. But looking after children can be intense, exhausting, exasperating – and sometimes suffocating! We mustn't push our own needs aside or feel guilty if we seek happiness in other ways too.

Research shows that your own psychological well-being impacts hugely on your ability to parent. It's vitally important to look after yourself just as you look after your child.

What will help and what is doable will be different for everyone. Sometimes the tiniest things can make a difference. It might be having a nap when your child naps or putting them in the buggy and going for a walk to get out of the house for a bit. It could be going for a half-hour run or going to a singing group in the evening. It could be getting up before your children wake up for a peaceful cup of tea on your own or getting away for a whole weekend.

Social contact and support, whether it be your partner, family or friends, has been shown to be key. Even a phone call with a friend or a chat to another parent pushing their child on the swing next to you can give you a boost.

Whatever you do, if you take care of your own separate 'self', you'll have more energy, patience, resilience, enthusiasm and clarity of mind to put into your parenting.

Relinquish control!

Some of us find it very difficult to leave our child with someone else – even our own partner. We worry our child won't manage without us and our way of doing things, e.g. 'They won't eat their toast if it isn't cut up into little triangles'. But children learn and accept very early on that different adults do things differently. So maybe your child didn't get their triangle toast – but that's because they made pancakes together instead! The time your child spends with your partner, a grandparent or someone else, improves their relationship which, in turn, will help you feel more relaxed about leaving them.

THE BIG PICTURE

Ideally, it's better if you can get the other significant grown-ups in your child's life on board with the advice in this book. But if you can't, don't worry. It won't 'undo' the good you're doing. Your children will still behave better with you!